SOME

TRUTHS

LIE

BENEATH

SOME

TRUTHS

LIE

BENEATH

REBECCA COLT ASLAN

atmosphere press

*This book is dedicated to the countless number of men and women
who have and will find a way to transcend sexual assault*

Foreword

When I was a teenager, I created a pen name for myself based on three of my favorite books—Rebecca Colt Aslan. Rebecca because I loved reading Daphne du Maurier, and her novel *Rebecca* was one of my favorites. Colt because my grandfather used to tell me about how I would sit on his lap reading a book about horses to him more times than he could count. I have loved horses all my life. Aslan because C. S. Lewis created a character who meant more to me than he could ever have imagined. I dreamt countless times of Aslan coming to rescue me.

I have chosen to use that pen name all these decades later because I do not want any of what caused me pain in my life to negatively impact my siblings or any others whom I may not be aware would find it difficult to process my truth. For that same reason, I have chosen to mask my profession as well.

Preliminary Reflections

Honestly, there are only two things I know for certain about life—the first unalterable fact is that I was born. The second truth of which I am certain is that I will die. Given the inevitability of death, I'm choosing to share some of the more troubling and hidden aspects of my history before my departure from Planet Earth. I hope that reading about my experiences will help someone as young and innocent as I once was glean something from them and avoid some of my pitfalls. It has been in the reading of others' lives that most of my positive choices have been born; perhaps my life can impact others in a way that, unbeknownst to them, countless other humans have done for me.

This won't read as a biography in the sense that I am not introducing personal details about my family (aside from experiences with my parents), career, or relationship milestones. I am trying to share only that which I need to convey my story of personal struggles, which remained almost one hundred percent internal. Throughout my life, all who have known me have seen a self-assured and happy persona. It's not that I haven't been happy, it's simply that I never shared my underlying intense pain. This began from a young age—for instance, my nickname from teachers in middle school was "Bubbles," yet I was crying myself to sleep every night, so much so that I needed to turn the pillow over because it would become oversaturated with my tears.

I am sixty-four years old and am content not to know exactly why I was so depressed as a child, although some of what I shall be sharing sheds a partial light. I am interested in living each day as it unfolds in the present, unencumbered by echoes of the past. I shall share some of those echoes here with the thought that reading about them may be of help in some way to a reader or two. Once shared, I will send them off into the ether.

And, now we travel back more than four decades...

Part 1: The Letter

Dear Rebecca,

The word "dear" that I just used is not merely a customary word as it is used to open a letter. I want you to know that I use it here in its deepest and truest meaning, for you are dear to me, as dear as any of the other children, and you always will be. Remember that as you read this letter and realize that everything I am about to say is said out of love for you, and because I am deeply concerned about your future and your happiness.

I had been dropped off at home after a Friday night out with friends. I was twenty years old and excited about heading back to college to complete my undergraduate degree after a year-and-a-half break and was filled with joy at the prospect of completing my degree. Enough of part-time jobs that would never provide a sustainable income—it was time I got back on track and established the beginning of a career in which I could support myself.

I walked in the back door and groggily climbed the three stairs to the kitchen entryway. We had a bulletin board just outside the kitchen where we could leave notes—this time I was greeted by an envelope tacked there with my name on it. My father's handwriting was unmistakable—so distinctive that it is still vivid in my mind. Seeing my name in his writing intrigued me. I didn't hesitate to hurry to my room to read what he had written.

My mom was a big letter writer once I went to college, but I had never received one from my dad before. Mom's letters always hurt. While my relationship with both parents was difficult, not for one second did I consider that my father's words would hurt more than all my mother's letters combined. I found myself looking forward to reading what he had taken the time to say.

As I sat on my bed, opening the envelope, I was certain that this had something to do with God answering my prayers. At that point in my life, I was deeply entrenched in Catholicism (long left behind after exposure to varied organized religions resolved into belief in none), and had recently attended a healing service facilitated by Father Ralph DiOrio in which I had prayed that *"things would get better at home, that I would feel comfortable as myself when I was there, and that you and Mom would like who I am."* I am only privy to this memory forty years later because I still retain the letter I wrote to my dad in response to the one being shared here.

Rereading those words to my father, I am reminded of my experience listening to Father DiOrio. When his service was over, he walked among the crowd, reaching out to touch people. I can recall where I was standing as if it were yesterday, and I can visualize him approaching my row as if I'm watching a scene in a movie. He reached over four or five people and gently touched my shoulder. At that moment I felt something invisible, but physically tangible, enveloping me as tears instantly began to stream down my face. I write these words after reflecting on that experience and find myself realizing that was the first and only time in my life I felt the safety of pure, unconditional love from another human being. As a very naïve twenty-year-old woman, I was certain that God had reached out through Father DiOrio to assure me that he would answer my prayers. Now, as a mature woman of sixty-four, I don't call it "God," but I do believe something in the universe touched me and opened me to something greater than myself.

What follows is not said for the purpose of negotiation, debate, or argument. It is said to let you clearly understand what both your mother's and my feelings are and what we have decided after long and agonizing consideration, discussion, and soul searching. It is not a statement of what you ought to do with your life, but rather a statement of what we are going to do with ours.

Lives can have pivotal moments, for sure, and reading my father's letter was one of those for me.

Your behavior and evolving attitudes over the last year and a half or so are what have brought me to the point of writing this letter. I will explain.

Before I let him explain, I would like to describe what led up to my sudden withdrawal from college only weeks before my junior year, which led to my living at home for the year and a half to which my father refers. Near the end of my sophomore year, I was out with many of my friends, listening to a musical group in which one of my professors was performing. The professor was pivotal in my academic growth, and I was filled with awe, respect, and admiration for him. When all my friends were ready to leave, my professor encouraged me to stay and enjoy the rest of the music—he assured me he would get me back to my dorm safely. The gesture made me feel extremely important and I readily accepted. I have no memory of my friends' opinions of this choice, but as an adult reflecting on it, I am acutely aware of the inappropriate nature of the invitation.

Let's explore my sexual and social development up to that point in my life to add context as to why I didn't think twice about leaving with this professor. I had little to no experience with boys or men. Throughout high school, I never had a date with anyone, but I frequently pined over specific boys I wished knew and cared about me. I had attended proms, but only with friends. In truth, the first and only date I ever went on was a few weeks before I left for college. It was with someone I thought was the most handsome and wonderful person I had ever met. I recall elation and anxiety as I readied myself for this date and have vivid memories of sitting across from him at dinner while feeling like the luckiest girl on the planet. All these years later, I can't even recall his name, but I can still see his wavy, sandy blond hair and beautiful, chiseled face. He was all my crushes rolled into one. He was in his early twenties, a local ski instructor, and friends with my boss at the corner deli where I had a part-time job. It was my boss who arranged for us to go on a date—most likely to humor me because I wouldn't stop talking about him every time he stopped in.

Before I share how the date ended, let me express some of my parents' teachings about sex and reproduction. I do this to shed light on the end of that date as well as many other things that occurred in my life.

At twenty, my parents had taught me that there was no purpose for sex other than procreation and that my role as a woman was to stop any man who tried to engage in sexual activity with me. My mother was adamant that men were unable to stop once they began, and it was up to me to ensure I never put myself in the position of being sexually alluring to a man. Her belief was so strong that when she saw my figure developing, she encouraged me to gain weight. Strange as it may sound, she was upset when she could see the definition of my collarbones. It was also strongly engrained in me that the use of any form of birth control (other than the natural rhythm method, which could be used during marriage) would ensure my place in hell and French kissing was a mortal sin.

One particularly disturbing example of my mother's preoccupation with eliminating my sexuality was the periodic inspection of my underwear in the laundry for signs of arousal—she would confront and humiliate me if she found what she considered to be an indication of such. My sexual understanding was so delayed that it wasn't until years later I understood what she was looking for. All books that had any indication of characters enjoying physical intimacy were taken from me with the explanation that I could not read anything that may trigger sexual desire until I was married and ready for children. With some manner of hypocrisy, my mom would give the books to her sister for my cousin, who was the same age as me, to read. At that time, I had complete trust in all that my parents taught in this area, which left me completely and utterly terrified of physical contact with men.

Now that I have shared that part of my history, perhaps you will understand my behavior at the end of my only date, as well as what is yet to unfold. I was on cloud nine as he walked me to the door but was shattered when he leaned in to kiss me. We were at my front door and fear enveloped me as I believed this was counter to all I had learned from my mother. As his lips touched mine, I recoiled as if he was the most repellant creature on earth. I can only imagine what he felt at my reaction as he mumbled something in a tone filled with disgust, turned, and walked away. The most magical night of my life had morphed into something utterly devastating and I stood there thinking I would never be able to stop crying.

The next day I tried to talk to my mother about it and couldn't help weeping as I did so. She simply advised me to dry my tears because they were evidence that I didn't have enough faith. My tears meant I was not accepting God's will in my life. She reminded me I was off to college in two weeks and recommended saying extra rosaries to accept what God ordained.

As many rosaries as I prayed, my experience of fear at the end of that date remained with me as I began my collegiate career and I began drinking heavily to compensate for my fear and anxiety. I had vowed never to drink alcohol after a lifetime of watching my parents' heavy drinking combined with an aunt's three DUIs. In my home, it was my job upon returning from school to mix my parents' Manhattans for the evening. I will never forget the Pyrex four-cup measuring container and the act of filling it with one cup of sweet vermouth, one cup dry, and two cups of whiskey. Even that wasn't enough for the two of them—after dinner they switched to Grand Marnier or Green Chartreuse for my father and Amaretto for my mother.

My vow not to follow in their footsteps with alcohol didn't last long. By week two of my freshman year, I was being carried back to my dorm, having become so inebriated that I was unable to walk. In retrospect, I am thankful that the boy who carried me home was a good friend of my roommate. I never went out without numbing myself with alcohol for many years to come— clearly, I did not understand that my parents' teachings about sexual intimacy had scarred me deeply. While undergraduate drinking is somewhat a rite of passage (especially at that time, since we had a bar on campus because the drinking age was only eighteen), I did not drink the way my peers did. Although I didn't realize it at the time, I did not drink simply to have fun with my friends. I did so with the sole purpose of becoming drunk enough to forget the pain of my past so I could interact socially with no emotional inhibitions. As a result, it would be years before I comprehended enough to seek help for how I was feeling.

I became terrified of interacting alone with a boy unless I was drunk at a party. It took no time at all to go from an avowed non-drinker to choosing to get a buzz before I went to any social gathering—if not, I couldn't even open my mouth to speak. Once, I agreed to go on a date with a kind and handsome boy from another college whom I met while drunk at a college mixer. When the time came for the date, I was experiencing too much anxiety to face him sober. When he arrived to pick me up, I asked my roommate to pick up the dorm phone and tell him I was sick. She ran back and said he was coming up to check on me. At that, I jumped into bed, we blew the hair dryer on my face on its hottest setting to make me look as if I had a fever, and I never heard from him again.

My sexual inexperience and prolific drinking continued, and I now return to the night my professor offered to drive me back to my dorm. I felt secure and cared for as I settled into the passenger seat, but was soon to learn that naïveté is not a helpful trait in college (or life in general).

"You certainly are horny tonight, aren't you?"

I recall turning my head and pressing my forehead onto the passenger side window, feeling frightened and confused—I didn't even know the meaning of "horny." My next memory is of a hand between my legs (thankfully over my jeans), rubbing and pushing so hard that it hurt while he kept saying, "Come on baby—you know you want it—relax." I squeezed my legs together, kept my head against the window, and prayed to get back to the dorm and out of the car. As the drive continued, he seemed frustrated that I remained frozen in place and moved his hand faster and harder. My pain and humiliation were overwhelming and once we reached the parking lot I jumped out of the car and ran to my dorm. When I reached my room, I fell to the floor in gut-wrenching sobs, and it was quite a while before my roommates could calm me down enough for me to tell them what had happened.

Thank goodness for caring friends. I felt safe again and, by the time I went to his class, I felt strong enough to say something to him about what he had done.

21

I sat in my preferred seat by the wall just inside the entrance to the classroom.

In all my classes, I liked to keep my back against the wall where I could see the entire class while remaining ready to make a quick exit. On this day, I remained in my seat until only myself and the professor remained. I gathered my resolve and, head held high, approached his desk.

"Why did you touch me like that?" I asked after class.

"Jesus Christ! You didn't tell anyone, did you? I would be crucified!" His response was so full of self-righteous anger and condemnation that I think I felt more frightened than I did when I was in his car. I had been swiftly put in my place and learned I needed to keep my mouth shut if I was to get through college.

While I had previously been drinking to feel comfortable in social situations, this experience added the "benefit" of escaping my emotions and memories. On one of the evenings when I was so inebriated at a dorm party that I could barely sit up, a boy came over, told me I was beautiful, and took my arm to take me upstairs with him. I had never felt attractive, and no one had ever said I was beautiful, so I was swept away by a feeling of being valued. Of course, I went with him—he was caring, kind, and made me feel safe. He took me into the upstairs bathroom and began kissing me. I was confused and shocked when I felt my jeans being undone and pulled down. It was then that I felt something very hard pushing against me, and a cautious understanding that this must be his erect penis entered my consciousness. I was filled with instant terror. That fear, combined with far too much alcohol resulted in an instant bout of vomiting. He immediately cursed and left while some girls I didn't know came and helped me. They told me he was a graduate student who had bragged to his friends that he was going to have sex with a stranger before he got married the following month. I was not equipped with the emotional strength to say "No," and remain thankful that my body took over and ended the encounter for me.

The incident with my professor and the one at the dorm party occurred near the end of my sophomore year. As much as I struggled with my parents, I found myself desperate for the year to end so I could be back at home and far away from life at college. I have no experiential memories of that summer except for one day in early August. I had told no one about having experienced sexual violations, but recurring thoughts of those incidents filled my days and nights. I recall standing at the mirror, blow-drying my hair and trying not to cry as I thought about returning to school. I could not imagine going back and having to see that professor again (he was scheduled to teach two of my classes) and I suddenly stopped the dryer and yelled out to anyone who was near, "I don't want to go back to school."

I suppose most parents would have had some questions about why their child was making this drastic statement out of the blue, but since mine only viewed college as an expensive means to gain a husband, they had no issues with that decision. When I reflect on how quickly they accepted that statement and moved forward with my withdrawal, I realize they were most likely delighted with my change of direction and the reason was of no consequence.

Oh, how drastically different my life would have been had they realized something must have happened for me to be saying I wanted to give up on a career to which I had been profoundly committed. I could speculate all I want on the infinite possible pasts I could have had, but at this moment as I write these words, I wouldn't have it any other way. I played the hand I was dealt and have yet to fold. My past is part of my story, but that is all. Simply a story that I hope might help others in some way.

And now, let's return to my bed and continue reading his letter as we "let my father explain."

Since you left college last year, you have become increasingly aloof from the family. While you have maintained varying degrees of physical presence at home, your emotional presence or your sense of belonging have steadily eroded, until now, home seems to exist for you solely as a hostel or way station, where there will be bed and board available at those times when your personal schedule is unable to be filled with any other activities.

Not only have you not participated in the family as a loving member, but you have shown increasing unwillingness to accept the obligations of a family member (of whatever age) to help around the house with those things that have to be done to maintain our home for the benefit of all the family members—yourself included. I refer to such things as shopping, cleaning, doing the dishes, running errands, etc. The result has been an increase in responsibility for those things not only on the other children, but especially on your mother.

Coupled with this decline in your participation in the obligations of family membership has been an increasing demonstration of your intent to "do your own thing" without regard for the feelings of or consequences to others. I could cite many examples of your inconsiderate behavior, but the purpose of this letter would not be served by that. I will just say that it is extremely difficult for your mother and me to understand how you learned to treat people like this.

Time sat still. I struggled to comprehend the words on the page. To whom could my father be referring? He was not home to see all that I did to help my mother in her role. I had much younger siblings and had been a partial mother to them their whole lives—had I not burned them years ago in a bonfire, I would share the words in my high school diaries where I detailed my role as a second mother while my friends were actively involved socially without me. Was this role to continue into my adulthood? Would there never be a time when I could live my own life? It never occurred to me at that time that, by remaining silent about my inner pain and turmoil, aspects of my personality may have shifted, leaving my father confused.

At the time I was reading my father's letter, I was set to continue my college education, having enrolled for the spring semester (I had found a way to avoid any courses taught by the professor by whom I had been violated). There was a new faculty member whom I had met during the past year while being involved on campus with my friends and she was instrumental in helping me find my way back to school. She had been to my home and had dinner with my parents as we worked out the details of my re-admittance. She wanted to do everything she could to help me complete my degree and forge a life for myself. This person was the first independent female I had met—someone living a life I had read about in books and saw on shows like Mary Tyler Moore, but never thought was realistic.

Lest you begin to question my sanity, recall that there was no such thing as social media and the internet when I was young. The only lives to which I was exposed were those approved by my parents. At that time, parents such as mine found it an easy task to shelter their children. Mine had kept our family in a very insular world consisting of church and home. Some of the less-than-kind neighborhood children referred to us as "caged kids" after my father fenced in our yard with a tall enough fence to block out the outside world.

Also, I want to express my thoughts (and your mother's) regarding your return to college this January. Given your financial conditions at the present time, and considering all other factors as well, we feel it is absolutely the wrong thing for you to do. Both your mother and I have made it clear to you that we feel you are saddling yourself with far too many loans to make your return to college in January a viable option. The obligations you will assume for this coming semester along with your existing obligations will mean you will owe about $7,000 with a year and a half of college yet to finance. (I can only imagine the gasps of incredulity of present-day readers whose typical college debt makes $7,000 seem like a pittance.)

You seem unalterably set on this course despite our warnings that you will graduate with total indebtedness of $10,000 or more and no prospect of a lucrative job. We both feel strongly—and we have made this known to you—that you should not return to college in January but should work full-time until you can save enough money for college so you can avoid going further into debt. Otherwise, when you graduate, you'll be saddled with loan payments that will eat up whatever salary you can make for years to come and seriously inhibit your ability to enjoy life as an individual or to get married and have a family.

And there it is—the only path acceptable for a young woman—"to get married and have a family." Truly, the part about enjoying "life as an individual" was not what mattered to my parents. My father taught me, regardless of my age, that I would be required

to do what he asked of me until I was married. Then, like all
virtuous women before me, I would take direction from my
husband.

My father was focused on the debt I would be accruing because, as he put it a couple of years later, "No man will ever want to marry you now that you are in debt." My father was nothing if not consistent as he demonstrated another decade later while watching me work on a research paper for my master's degree: "Do you know what it feels like to know that I will likely go to my grave knowing my eldest daughter is a spinster?"

The living arrangements you contemplate in college are also totally unacceptable to us. I am sure that your living arrangement with a professor will cause much grief for you, alienation of your peers, and embarrassment for her. Yet nothing we say is able to deter you from your intentions.

The professor to whom he refers is the one who befriended me during my time away from school; the one whom they had invited to dinner only a few weeks prior, where she explained to them that she was happy to let me stay with her on weekdays during the semester so I wouldn't have to pay for room and board. She considered it to be a "paying it forward" of sorts because she believed in my potential.

So, knowing this, and knowing that you are an adult woman of almost twenty-two years of age, your mother and I have decided to take the following course in the conduct of our lives and in consideration of those lives for whom we are still responsible—your younger brothers and sisters:

We are going to devote all our parenting and resources to those children who are our responsibility. Your desire for self-expression and your physical presence in the family without a corresponding contribution to the functioning of the family is too detrimental. The concern and attention that this situation demands of us are making it impossible for us as parents to do our job with your younger brothers and sisters.

So, after considering all of the alternatives, we have decided that you will have to pursue your life apart from the rest of the family. We feel it will be best for everyone—especially for you—to get away from home to do whatever you decide to do. I said in the second paragraph of this letter I'm not telling you what to do with your life. You can do whatever you want, but you're going to have to do it totally on your own so that it doesn't interfere with the lives of the rest of us.

Being practical about the situation, we certainly don't expect you to leave until you can make satisfactory arrangements to live somewhere else. Believe me, Rebecca, it is not easy for me to say this, but I am painfully aware that there is no other way. It is apparent to both your mother and me that our influence in your life has run its course. If anything, we are now in some way an unhealthy influence in your life. So in closing I'll make some suggestions to you:

Seek some objective, unbiased, professional guidance in your decision-making regarding your life.

Get away from college and home so you can make some independent decisions uncolored by the emotions these surroundings produce.

Get a job and support yourself completely for a while before you do anything else.

Pray and stay close to God and His Blessed Mother and ask their help in sorting out your life. Remember, it is God who has given you the tremendous intellect you have. Surely, He will guide you to the best way to use your mind for His honor and glory—if you let Him.

Finally, Rebecca, I'll say again, I love you and I want the best for you. You are always welcome here. Don't interpret this letter as if I'm throwing you out of the house. I'm not! I'm telling you I know your "wings" are strong and it's time you "flew out of the nest" on your own for your own good no matter how uncomfortable or frightening you may think that prospect is. I am also telling you that if you continue to remain here, it will be bad not only for you, but you will be inhibiting the growth and development of the other "fledglings" who live here who are not yet ready to "fly."

God bless you. I love you.

Dad

Sitting cross-legged on my bed, barely seeing the pages through a waterfall of tears in the middle of the night while the rest of the house slept in peace, these isolated words physically reverberated inside my skull:

Don't interpret this letter as if I'm throwing you out of the house.

At the time, I knew of no other way to interpret that letter. All I knew was that this was a man, who, while frequently hard on me, I had trusted to be the voice of reason in response to my mother's emotional diatribes—that man wafted into oblivion during the reading of his letter. In the numb shock of the moment, all I could think about was getting out before I completely self-destructed.

Up until that moment, there had been many times throughout my high school years when I sat in the locked bathroom contemplating suicide—holding a razor blade against my wrists with the undying desire to disappear from the planet. I recall stopping myself with thoughts that it would mean my mother had won. What would I do to myself in that home with the new belief that I didn't have either of my parents in my corner? I sat on my bed and wept until the first light of morning, before anyone had awoken, and called the friend who had dropped me off the night before. I sobbed and begged her to come pick me up and couldn't even explain why. Memory is fascinating because I recall waiting outside my home for her, but I don't remember leaving the house or what I brought with me except for the letter. I do know that I said nothing to anyone, did not leave a note, and we went to McDonald's.

I sat across from her as she read the letter and felt a kind of relief when I saw that it made her cry and feel sad as well. So, I wasn't crazy to be hurt... Perhaps I didn't handle the situation very well by simply leaving, but it seemed that was what my dad wanted me to do. It was the only message I was able to glean from his letter. That, and I was a horrible person not worthy of living in his home unless I was willing to be someone different. All these years later with the benefit of hindsight and conversations with my father before he passed away, I know he only wanted the best for me, and he didn't know how to accomplish that. He and my mother did the best they could. It's just a fact of life that sometimes a person's best can be devastating for someone else.

I stayed at my friend's house that weekend and, since we had already planned to attend a weekend lecture given by the professor who was helping me return to school, we went. My friend was aware that I was going to be staying with that professor (whom I will begin to refer to as Dr. Taylor for the sake of her privacy) during the week once our semester began and, unbeknownst to me, she approached her about my situation.

Dr. Taylor came to me immediately following her lecture and extended an invitation for me to stay with her as long as I liked, and I thankfully accepted her offer. I borrowed a friend's car (because mine was parked in my parents' driveway, totaled after a recent accident) and returned to my home early Monday morning to pick up necessities and move to Dr. Taylor's apartment.

39

I believe the timing of my father's letter was not a coincidence as it came within a week of my car being totaled and he knew I did not yet have enough money for repairs. In his mind I was "stranded" and would not be able to leave, so I would have no other choice than to follow the directions he had laid out for me. One of his goals was to keep me from Dr. Taylor, and the opposite was achieved.

Part 2: After the Letter

Before we move on, let me offer the letter I wrote to my father in response to his. While I might say some things differently forty years later, my words then represent who I was at the time. If I remember correctly, I mailed this letter about a week after leaving:

Dear Dad,

This letter will not win any prizes for its literary potential, but I hope it may make you understand me a little.

I know you were hurt and upset when I didn't talk to you about your letter, and when I left so soon, but I don't know if you could ever comprehend the feelings I experienced after reading it. After realizing what you thought of me and what I plan to do with my future, I knew there was nothing to say. Everything came as such a shock that there was no way I could talk sensibly about it. I have never felt comfortable saying anything I feel at home, which is why it always comes out so screwed up and jumbled, but this time I couldn't even defend my decisions or myself as a human being because I never realized until I read your letter what a basically screwed-up person you think I am.

Dad, I'm used to hearing things like that from Mom because I know and have known ever since I was a junior in high school that she doesn't understand what's inside me, but I always felt you had a special understanding of me. After I read your letter, I think I went into shock—if that's what being totally emptied of all feeling is called. I couldn't cope with what you said; therefore, I couldn't discuss it. There was also no way I could stay home knowing what you think of me. I know you said you love me, and I believe it logically, but I also know logically that if I believed about another human being the things you wrote about me, I would find it very difficult to love that person—even if she was my daughter.

I don't know how to make you understand me, but I know what I'm doing is not wrong—and neither is the way I'm doing it. My friends have seen me change my mind even more than you have, yet when I explain how excited I am about going back to school and choosing this career path, they believe me because they understand what's in my heart and in my mind. One person who had absolutely nothing to do with my decision is Dr. Taylor. The only reason we became friends was, after I decided to go back to college, I saw her as a person who could help me. I introduced myself and told her what I've done and what I plan to do. Maybe the only way I can make you understand is to do it—because boy am I going to do it! (I ultimately "did it," but "boy" that last phrase is embarrassing...)

I'm also not doing anything wrong by staying with Dr. Taylor. She sees in me a special ability and she wants to do all she can to help me realize my potential. She also knows that were I in her position and I met someone like myself, I would do the same thing and expect nothing in return except dedication to everything that was being provided. Maybe you don't understand that and maybe I didn't explain it very well, but it's the best I can do.

Mom keeps telling me how much I've hurt everyone as if I'm not supposed to be hurt by the way you both feel. I feel like you want me to become a totally new person with a brand-new beginning. That's not what I want because

I've already sorted out in my head what I want. Believe me, nothing hurts more than having your parents be the only two people who don't believe you. I love you both and respect your feelings too much not to be hurt when you won't accept my decisions. I'm not a little kid and, in the past year out of college, I've done a lot of learning about myself. Unfortunately, I haven't let you or Mom see it, and that, I believe, is where our problems lie.

Whenever I was home, I was not myself because I was afraid to be. Mainly because I know I haven't turned out to be exactly what—or who—you want me to be. I am very different inside than you or Mom. I used to think that was bad, which is what screwed me up at home. Now, for the first time, I feel really good about myself and what I'm doing. It's because I realize there is nothing that says I have to think, act, and behave as my parents. I honestly don't believe that makes me a bad person, either. I pray that now, with me not being home, I can show you that I have become my own person and I am not as bad as you think. I've never given you a chance to know me on the inside. Maybe now I'll be able to. I believe things will get better between us because they've already been at the worst, which only leaves room for improvement.

When I went to Father DiOrio's service, I put in the petition that things would get better at home, that I would feel comfortable as myself when I was there, and that you and Mom would like who I am. That's why when he touched me, I was so moved (and that's why I really couldn't talk about it to you at that time). I felt that God would help make things better. Then when I got your letter, I lost all faith, but it's starting to come back because I think this is the way it will get better. Things would keep getting worse if I stayed home and I guess we both know that. I think God had to let things get to the lowest point they could before he could start building them up again.

I really love you and will do everything I can to show you who I really am.

Thanks for being my dad!

Love,

Rebecca

I can only speculate as to how my father felt reading that letter because we never spoke about it. As far as my relationship with my family went after I left, my siblings were not allowed to see me outside of our family home for years. I never reestablished any semblance of a relationship with my mother before she died twelve years later when I was thirty-three. Even though I had been in counseling for the decade before her death, I was still filled with hurt and anger toward her and my father. It is without shame that I share my feeling of joy when I heard she had passed away, although my anger underwent a powerful transformation when I stood in front of her casket at the funeral home. In this moment as I type, I can still see her calm, relaxed expression—the only time I ever saw her look at peace. I stared at her, devoid of care but exhausted from my anger, and whispered to her serene presence, "Please take my anger with you." It is thirty years after her passing, and I have yet to feel the type of anger with which I had been living. I did not and do not mourn my mother because I did not and do not miss her. What I did and sometimes still mourn, however, is a mother's unconditional love.

Please understand that my experience with my parents was mine alone. I don't speak for any of my siblings and was confused when I saw tears of sadness from them at my mother's funeral. Both of my parents had wonderful qualities and loved all their children. It's just that my mother's love for me never felt real. She and my father had such a strong desire for me to fit the mold they shaped for me that they could not accept me for who I was.

Shortly after my mother died, I was to learn that my father understood this. Within a week of my mother's passing, my father called and asked if I would come over to have dinner with him. He said he wanted to understand why I remained so alienated from the family. I told him I would have dinner with him only if he promised to listen without judgment. To my surprise, he readily acquiesced, so I accepted his offer with guarded hope. I knew he truly wanted these answers, because a few years before my mother's death, my father unexpectedly showed up at my workplace. He said he had come to find out why I did not come home more often, and I said I would talk to him about it but needed him to keep it between us. He told me, regretfully, that he could not promise that because there was nothing he would keep from my mother. I truly admired the depth of his love and devotion to her but could not share anything personal because I did not trust my mother's emotional response. I feared what was already difficult between us would become even more unbearable should she hear "my side." With my mother's passing, that concern was moot, and I was curious to see if I could reestablish a relationship with my father. I had long since learned from a sibling that the letter he had written was done so at the prompting of my mother—she could certainly be quite persuasive—and by then, with the help of time and therapy, I held no animosity toward him. I missed him in my life.

While my father's letter from years before became a pivotal life moment, so did this dinner. True to his word, I was able to outline, without interruption, all the reasons I had stayed away—I expressed that whenever I came to visit after I moved out, I was met with emotional and intense criticism from my mother. She would berate my father if he showed interest in my life—I reminded him of one visit when he and I were speaking together on the porch and my mother came out screaming (not hyperbole) that he should not be asking me anything about myself because I didn't care enough to come home more often. I recalled for him another visit: sitting with my mother at the dining room table, having a rare, seemingly innocuous conversation, when she announced to younger siblings who were present that I was an example of what they should never aspire to be. She asked me to leave, saying that my presence made it harder for her to raise my siblings. I reminded him of the time I came home for my grandmother's funeral (my father's mother, whom I loved deeply), and I was humiliated in front of the many extended family members who were there when my mother erupted at my presence.

My father listened to all I had to say and thanked me for painting the picture for him. He told me that he and my mother had never allowed my younger siblings to visit me because I wasn't a practicing Catholic. They were concerned I would have been a negative influence in their lives. It was during this dinner that my father realized they had been wrong to make that decision and he genuinely apologized. After dinner, I was looking at the plethora of loving cards sent to my father from the many people who mourned my mother's death. Card after card described a kind and loving woman who would be deeply missed. I held one of the cards and murmured to my father, "You do know I never met that woman?" We both kept our eyes on the cards, and he gently replied, "I know."

Part 3: Final Violations

I was twenty-one years old when I moved out and became hyper-focused on establishing a career. As time passed, I drifted away from every friend I ever had. I was to be a bridesmaid at the wedding of the wonderful friend who picked me up after I received my father's letter—I even had the dress—and I made an excuse as to why I couldn't attend. I failed to attend the wedding of the college roommate whom I loved. While I have foggy memories of that time, as my career gained momentum, I am certain I caused hurt and confusion to many people.

By the time I was thirty-three (the same age I was when my mother passed away), my career was at a turning point, and I was appointed a supervisor in my workplace who would help propel me up the ladder. I trusted him as a mentor, and he told me that to move up in the company I would have to be open with him about my personal life. He explained the necessity for him to know the details so there were no surprises once I was promoted. Seriously? I know how foolish it was to think that was true, but as my trusted and respected mentor, I believed him.

Here's a classic example of what I should have understood as manipulation, but which simply flattered me: The first thing he wanted to know was how someone as beautiful as me wasn't married. Bells and whistles should have been resounding in my head, but I believed his words were innocent because he was a happily married man. I chose to explain that I was not interested in establishing a relationship because I didn't want to be deterred from the path I was on. I had become very independent and self-reliant—something for which I felt a lot of pride. It's hard to explain how safe and respected I felt with him, combined with how motivated I was to move up in the company, so I told him the truth about my life of chosen celibacy.

And now we come to the last two horrible sexual experiences I have left to describe.

My supervisor told me that a mentally healthy individual couldn't live life without sex and he had concerns that I might not be stable enough to even remain with the company, let alone be promoted. We were in his office and he told me he was going to prove how much I needed it so I could make a better decision about my personal life. He said my career would never go anywhere if I remained celibate because he would need to note in my file concerns about mental health issues. He also made it very clear that I would be unemployable in the field since he was the point of first contact for any future employer should I decide to look elsewhere. He then grabbed me and kissed me so hard that it hurt. I was shocked, weaker than him, and unable to get out of his grip. He kept one hand behind my head and the other grabbing my left breast. I know it was my left breast because the pain was excruciating and will never be forgotten. He let me go and told me to go home and think about how much I needed more of that. Another aspect of that experience that will never be forgotten is what I saw when I looked in the mirror after a shower. My entire left breast was bruised pitch-black. I have had severe bruising from falls off my mountain bike, none of which came close to the ebony black of the bruises covering my breast. I honestly didn't think it would ever return to normal.

Since I said "last two," I shall share something I have told few people about and written about only twice—once to the human resource manager at my workplace after becoming fortunate enough to find other employment and once to my current boyfriend during our initial "getting to know each other" email exchanges almost twenty years ago. Honestly, I hate writing it not because I can't handle it but rather because I don't want anyone else to have to ponder the reality. Trust me, I didn't cope well for many years and can still be triggered, but now I write it only out of hope that my words may help others understand predatory behavior.

While I shared information about my upbringing and my father's letter—not to shed blame on my parents but to point out the power parental figures sometimes inadvertently use to weaken the humans placed in their care—I share what follows to demonstrate that some people wield their power with conscious malicious intent. If anyone reading this feels controlled by any teachings or intentions that differ from what is in your core as a human, you do not have to follow them. That's all I wished I could have known. I let things I was taught stay deep inside and chain me into weakness and susceptibility to anyone in power. First to my parents, second to the undergraduate professor described earlier, third to the boy whom I let manipulate me into the bathroom when I was inebriated, and lastly to this supervisor of whom I now speak.

My supervisor assigned me to attend a conference shortly after the experience in his office. I was relieved to get out of town and regroup. Getting out of town was accomplished, but regrouping was not. I answered a knock on my hotel room door and foolishly failed to look through the peephole. Pushing his way in, he snarled, "I'm here to finish what I started."

How could this be? What did this mean? My bruised breast wasn't yet healed, and the monster was now inside my hotel room. Despite all protestations, I was thrown on the bed and he had his way with me in every sexual manner except for anal penetration.

That is all I will write to describe the experience other than to say I dissociated from my body as it occurred. That happened twenty-seven years ago, and I began working on this piece four years ago knowing it would end with a rape. As I type these words, I am acutely aware of why it has taken me four years to finish this task. I was left virtually comatose on the bed, and he left my room stating, "This stays between us or I will ruin you."

I need to describe what happened next in the hopes of helping people understand that a human can be brutalized by rape and function on the outside as if nothing has taken place. I had a presentation at the conference that evening and had to get ready. I'd like to be able to describe my emotions or thoughts from the time, but it is impossible. Perhaps it is a gift of my unconscious that I cannot recall because truly nothing remotely as viscous has occurred before or since. The sexual violations I experienced when I was younger were trivial compared to this. Please understand I say that not to minimize those awful experiences to which far too many women are subject, but to highlight the chasm for me between the trauma of what took place when I was younger and this rape.

I took a shower, got dressed, prepared my materials, and went to do my presentation. "He" was in the first row, engaged and in control, asking questions and taking notes. I gave a presentation of which seasoned professionals would have felt proud but have no idea what came out of my mouth. I visualized myself pointing and saying over and over, "He raped me this afternoon." That's clearly not what I said because that presentation changed my future. After it was over, my supervisor approached me with an attendee from another company who was making an offer to hire me. "She's done a great job for us, but I would never want to hold her back. It's your decision, Rebecca." He stared at me intensely; I knew what it meant, and I scheduled a meeting to talk with the man who was to become my new employer.

The guilt I felt at not reporting what happened carried a weight I still feel to this day. I was seeing a counselor at the time and never even told her. In fact, she felt I was doing so well that she questioned my need to continue, and I stopped. Hence, *some truths lie beneath*. No one can get them out of another person until they are ready. I am hoping my truth will facilitate a greater understanding of the trauma created by sexual assault. I told no one what happened to me and somehow, a full year later, I found myself finally telling my best friend. I lost all control emotionally as if it was happening all over again when I finally said the words out loud. I'm detached from the pain three decades later, but to this day I cannot read or watch anything that hints at even the mildest sexual violation. It also remains painful to hear to this day—even with the strength of the #MeToo movement—people questioning the validity of an accusation if the accuser waited any length of time to tell what happened. The pain of rape is something I would never wish on any man or woman, but the understanding of its repercussions is vital. Honestly, I think that is one reason I am writing this.

I did do one thing to try and find some semblance of justice. I wrote a detailed account of everything that had taken place with my supervisor and took it to the director of human resources before I left. That visit is one memory I can vividly recall. I asked him if I could turn something in anonymously and he assured me I could but said he may not be able to do anything without a name attached. I explained that I was far too afraid of the repercussions should I go public. (If you are one of the many questioning my decision, remember this was 1993—only two years after I watched every second of Anita Hill be demeaned, judged, and misbelieved by members of Congress for describing sexual harassment at the hands of Judge Clarence Thomas. I could only imagine the response if she had been describing a rape.)

I sat across his desk while the director of human resources read through my statement. He was very still and, upon finishing, he reached for one of his desk doors and pulled out a file. "Now I can let the bastard go." He explained that mine was the third anonymous report and while he couldn't file legal charges on that basis, he could now let him go—two had not been enough. He told me each previous allegation had been vehemently denied, and he used his decade-long marriage and young children as evidence of his character. Not to mention that he was highly respected in the field. I never followed up to see where he went, but still have guilt knowing that it is most likely he has caused other women to suffer in the same manner. I hold onto a smidgen of hope he had been scared straight after losing his job. In my mind, three anonymous reports mean far more were impacted, and I say that knowing how difficult it was to come forward even though I was not allowing my name to be associated with my experience. I am acutely aware that the actual statistics regarding sexual assault are most likely significantly higher than reported. As I think about women I have known in my life, more than seventy-five percent have experienced some sort of sexual violation, and three that I know of have been raped without ever reporting it. All the women I know were violated by men they knew and trusted. I am only one woman in a sea of billions on this earth and can only imagine how many more unreported violations have taken place.

Part 4: Moving On

A couple of years after my rape, I started to think about how I didn't want my last sexual encounter before death to be a violent one. I spoke to my sister about it, and she recommended joining a dating website. I took her advice—since I didn't want to be in a relationship, I stated I wasn't looking for a commitment. Those words opened a Pandora's box of penis images.

If you want to be quickly soured about the future of relationships given the ease of internet connections, do what I did. I received well over a hundred truly nauseating penis images within the first twenty-four hours of uploading my profile seeking "no commitment," and more poured in every day. The majority of the men responding to my profile were married and not hiding that fact. I didn't even have a picture of myself, yet all of these men would have agreed to meet for sex with me at any time or place I chose. I will never understand why men think women are attracted to them simply by looking at their penis. As the images continued to arrive in my inbox, I began to think I was a fool for trying to have a sexual relationship.

One day, as I was enjoying an extended vacation, I looked through the dating website to see if there was anyone local and I was drawn to an image of a man standing under a tree by a lake. He looked so kind and unassuming. I don't even recall what was in his profile besides that—he was simply the first man I had seen with a real picture and seemingly no pretense. I chose to reach out to him, and my brilliant message was something like, "Are you horny? I am."

Honestly, that's what I thought men needed to hear to be interested in a woman. I suppose the phrase remained in my subconscious from my time with the professor in the car. I may have been forty-four years old at the time, but, aside from a couple of consensual and meaningless flings, I had only ever been on that one date described from back when I was eighteen, sexually violated a couple of times, and raped. I knew nothing about truly good men and relationships.

To my surprise, the unassuming man under the tree responded with no reference to my statement. We began chatting in the chat room of the website and had a wonderful conversation. It was the first time I realized emotions could be elicited from simple words being typed back and forth on a screen. Michael made me laugh and it felt wonderful. Since we were only an hour apart, we decided to meet at a restaurant halfway. I had a feeling like none other as I watched him glide past the window of the restaurant in which I was waiting. We talked for hours as if we had known each other our whole lives. We went back to my place where he spent the night and I had my first experience of meaningful sex. I knew, even though my actual home and job were six hours away, I would find a way to keep this man in my life.

After that, Michael and I communicated via email multiple times a day, spoke for hours on the phone every night, and became more and more connected. I shared more about my life with Michael than I ever had with anyone—think of all the money I spent on counseling, and yet no counselor ever heard half of the personal details I shared with him. I was feeling truly happy for the first time in my life. Michael wanted nothing more from me than the brief times we could be together, and I did not have to leave my life, home, and job. This evolved into weekend visits for the next seventeen years while no weekday passed without spending time on the phone. Three years ago, I retired, and, as we enjoy the twentieth year of our relationship, we are living happily in the home we share.

Parting Thoughts

Please love yourselves, love others, and don't judge. We are all humans trying to survive on this planet called Earth and each one of us deserves to live free of the dictates of other humans or institutions. I recently heard Eckhart Tolle say, "You are what you're looking for." He is so right. Don't let anyone cause you to feel less than that. People who inflict any type of pain are living in pain—don't internalize theirs. You have the power to rise above. They have truths that lie beneath as well—they simply haven't faced them.

Be well.

About Atmosphere Press

Founded in 2015, Atmosphere Press was built on the principles of Honesty, Transparency, Professionalism, Kindness, and Making Your Book Awesome. As an ethical and author-friendly hybrid press, we stay true to that founding mission today.

If you're a reader, enter our giveaway for a free book here:

SCAN TO ENTER
BOOK GIVEAWAY

If you're a writer, submit your manuscript for consideration here:

SCAN TO SUBMIT
MANUSCRIPT

And always feel free to visit Atmosphere Press and our authors online at atmospherepress.com. See you there soon!

About the Author

REBECCA COLT ASLAN lives a quiet and peaceful life with Michael, her partner of twenty years. She is an avid tennis player and loves to sit outside reading, listening to birds, and watching wildlife. Having eclectic interests, she loves playing games like Borderlands and Forza 5 on her X-Box, listening to Science Fiction and Fantasy novels, as well as watching all genres of streaming series. In addition, now that she is retired, she loves never having to worry about dressing for work or setting her alarm.

Ms. Aslan proudly wears this tattoo on her arm as a reminder of strength and resilience.

If you wish to discuss anything with the author
after reading this book, you may email Ms. Aslan
at rebeccacoltaslan@gmail.com

Ms. Aslan welcomes correspondence.

It is difficult to struggle alone. While you can always search for local resources, here are a few national resources to use as a starting point:

National Sexual Violence Resource Center
nsvrc.org

Rape, Abuse and Incest National Network (RAINN)
rainn.org

National Institute on Alcohol Abuse and Alcoholism
niaaa.nih.gov

Substance Abuse and Mental Health Services
Administration
samhsa.gov